WRITE AHEAD 3
Write again

Hello! I'm Pen.

And I'm Nib.

TOM BARNARD

Osmiroid • MACMILLAN

© Osmiroid International Ltd and
Macmillan Education Ltd 1989

All rights reserved. No reproduction, copy or transmission
of this publication may be made without written permission.

No paragraph of this publication may be reproduced, copied
or transmitted save with written permission or in accordance
with the provisions of the Copyright Act 1956 (as amended),
or under the terms of any licence permitting limited copying
issued by the Copyright Licensing Agency, 33–4 Alfred Place,
London WC1E 7DP.

Any person who does any unauthorised act in relation to
this publication may be liable to criminal prosecution and
civil claims for damages.

First published 1989

Published by
MACMILLAN EDUCATION LTD
Houndmills, Basingstoke, Hampshire RG21 2XS
and London
Companies and representatives
throughout the world

and
Osmiroid International Limited
Fareham Road
Gosport
Hampshire PO13 0AL

Phototypeset by Gecko Limited, Bicester, Oxon

Designed by
The Design Works, Reading

Illustrated by Juliet Breese

Printed in Hong Kong

ISBN 0–333–47074–5

Note for parents and teachers

Write ahead! is a three-book handwriting revision series. If a child has problems with handwriting, these three books will help him or her to start again, and quickly form good habits which will lead to legible and fast writing.

- Book 1 (*Making letters*) goes back to basic letters, to make sure that the child is forming them correctly. It is essential that the child should start each letter in the right place, and make the movements in the right direction.
- Book 2 (*Joining up*) practises joining letters and forming words correctly. This is essential if the child is to write fast and legibly.
- Book 3 (*Write again*) gives more practice in fast and fluent writing. It practises writing for different purposes; it encourages children to write imaginatively but still neatly; and it encourages them to enjoy handwriting as an art form.

The style practised is the Basic Modern Hand. This is a popular, standard style especially well suited to fast writing. The alphabet is taught from the beginning with a slight leaning to the right, and with small exit strokes to prepare for the joining stage.

These books can be used at home, or to consolidate work being done at school. They can largely be worked through by children on their own, though slower readers may need help from an adult from time to time. You might also like to discuss the illustrations and activities with your child.

Pages 4 to 7 give more detailed information on using the books. You will need to check that the child is following these instructions correctly. Provide plenty of plain paper for extra practice.

How to use this book

Hello!
This book is called <u>Write again</u> and it's the third of three books called <u>Write ahead</u>. The first book was a reminder about how to make all the letters of the alphabet in the best and fastest way. The second book practised joining different letters together to make words.

This book gives you plenty of practice for different jobs. There are lots of examples for you to trace and copy. First of all you can trace or copy in the book. Then you can practise on separate sheets of paper, or in your own special book. These symbols show you what to do:

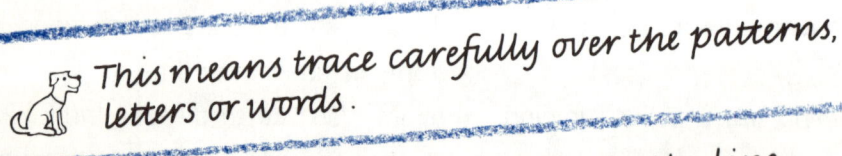

- This means trace carefully over the patterns, letters or words.

- This means copy the exercise on the line provided.

- This means go on practising on separate paper or in a special book. Page 7 has lines for you to use for writing on.

- 60 secs — This means test your writing speed in the time it says. Practise on a separate sheet of paper <u>fast</u>. Make sure your writing stays clear. Did the letters start in the right place? Did you go round the right way? Have a good look.

In the first part of this book, there is a bit of revision of writing quickly and neatly, using this alphabet. Can you remember which letters join up, and which can be left unjoined?

abcdefghijklmnopqrstuvwxyz

Then you will think about the different ways we can write. For example, when making lists you can write quickly and don't have to be quite so neat. When you write letters you need to be very neat, so that the person you are writing to can read what you have put in the letter. There are also pages about writing notices and invitations, and decorating them, making badges and labels, and designing covers for books.

Now that you can write well you could look at different sorts of pen. Try writing your name with a ball pen, a roller ball writer, a fibre tip pen and a fountain pen.

_____
ball pen

_____
roller ball

_____
fibre tip

_____
fountain pen

Which looks best? Which is easiest to use? Give them points out of 10.

ball pen   roller ball   fibre tip   fountain pen

Later on, you could try out different pens for making patterns and swirls. Good luck and have fun!

Pen and 🐾 Nib

A few reminders

Hold the pen lightly. Don't grip it too hard.

Make sure you have good lighting. Bright daylight or a strong lamp are best.

Make sure you are sitting comfortably. Don't bend over the table.

When you are testing the speed of your writing, you should aim for 70 letters per minute. Don't expect to write this fast straight away, though. Start slowly and carefully, and build your speed up.

Are you left handed?

If you are left handed, you will find that you are rubbing your hand across your writing. You can't see what you are doing, and you may make lots of smudges.

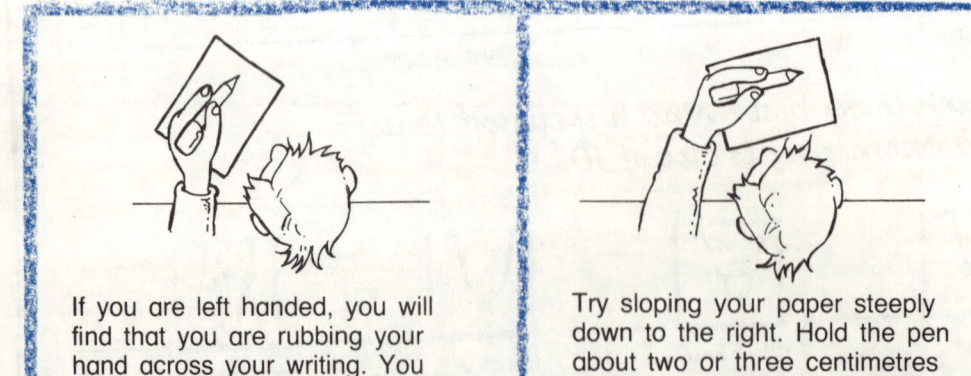

Try sloping your paper steeply down to the right. Hold the pen about two or three centimetres from the tip. Now you should be able to see what you are doing, and not make smudges.

Clip a sheet of paper over this page. Trace the lines onto your paper carefully. Then, when you want to practise writing, clip the lined sheet under the paper you are writing on.

Fit your letters into the spaces like this:

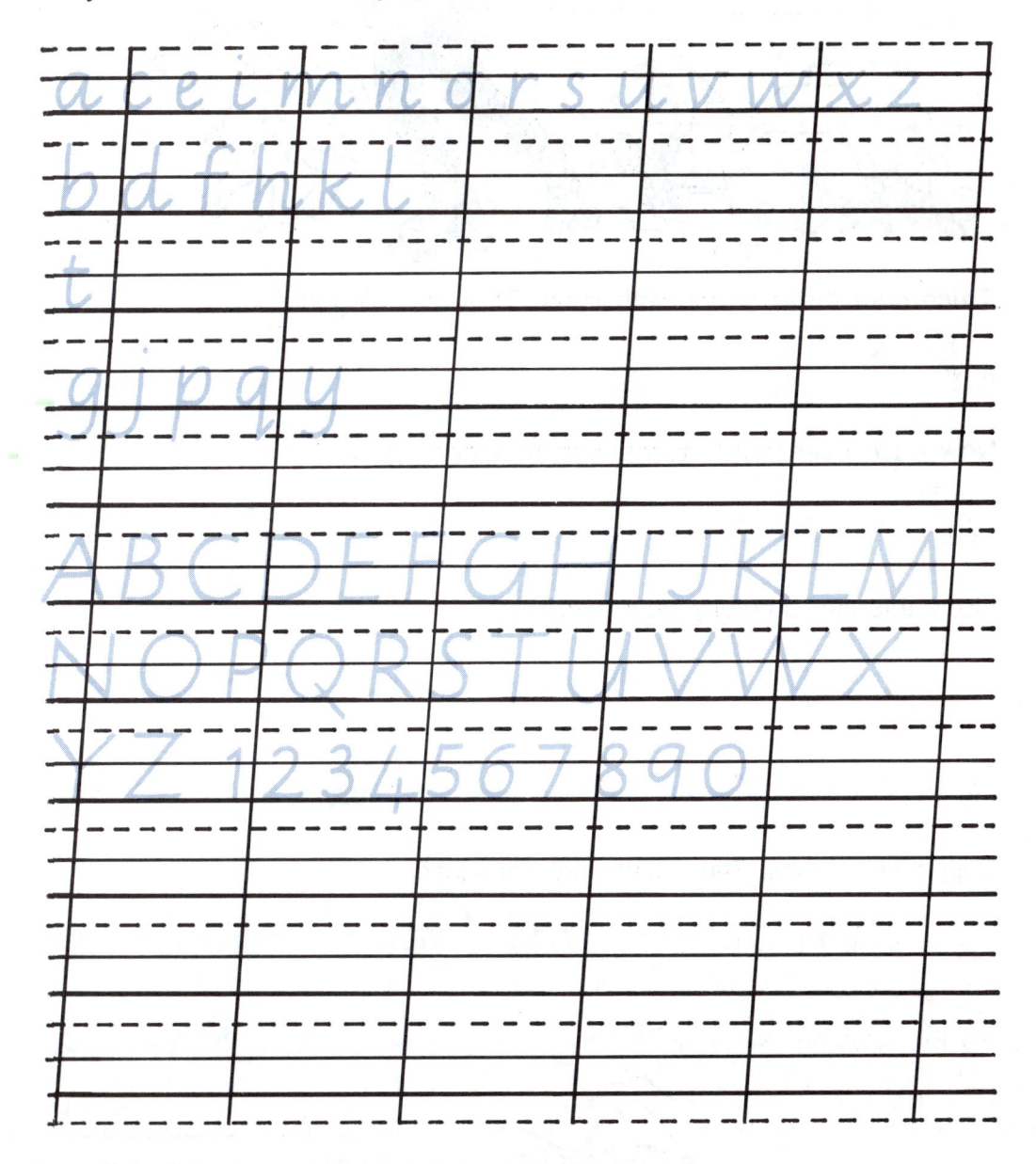

aeimnorsuvwxz
bdfhkl
t

gjpqy

ABCDEFGHIJKLM
NOPQRSTUVWX
YZ1234567890

"Look at these joins. They glide smoothly, and turn cleanly, just like me!"

"Look where you're going, Pen!"

Trace over these words with joins. They are diagonal joins.

Nine nuns run willy-nilly

Now trace over these words with horizontal joins.

A bowl of oats is for good food

Copy this line carefully underneath.

Granny grows giant gooseberries.

Granny grows giant gooseberries

Copy these names. The capitals are not joined.

Ben Jody Tom Heidi Paul Jan

Ben Jody Tom Heidi Paul Jan

There are some letters we don't join from. They are

b g j p q s x y z

8

Be careful with your joins.
It's easier not to join from some letters.
Can you see which ones?
They are marked with dots.

Try using an **f** with a long stroke.

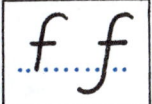

f f

Copy the joined alphabet as neatly as you can.

abcdefghijklmnopqrstuvwxyz

Copy this line carefully underneath.

five furry fluffy foxes following fourteen fantastic frogs.

We do not join from capitals or numbers.

ABCDEFGHIJKLMNOPQR
STUVWXYZ 0123456789

Trace over these, and then copy them carefully underneath.

Elizabeth Michael Sarah John

Some words flow on and on. You can join most of these letters onto the next one.

Trace over this sentence and practise writing it on your own.

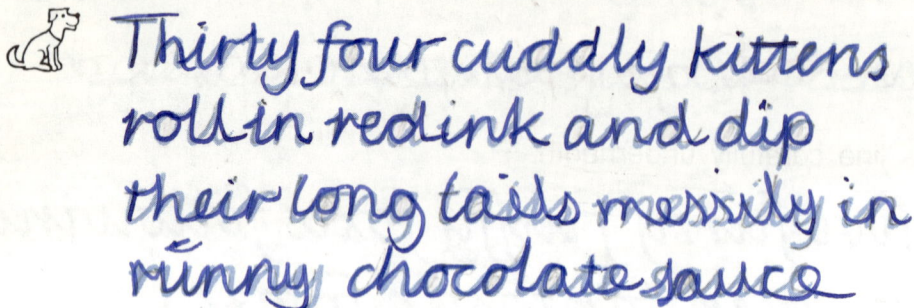

Thirty four cuddly kittens roll in red ink and dip their long tails messily in runny chocolate sauce

Here are some more flowing words. Use them to write some silly sentences.

nip holiday on takes at coach two cuddle with fun came the home decide animal lemonade dance meanwhile voice meal chocolate waving announce or months

Here's one to start you off.

Remember! Don't join from capital letters!

The coach holiday takes two months with no lemonade.

Practise with flowing words until you can write them neatly and quickly. Use the line guide on page 7.

Copy this sentence slowly.

The fox rode loudly down the hill, did a few wheelies up and down the town, and went home for his cocoa and cake.

The fox rode loudly down the hill, did

Now practise writing the sentence on a separate sheet of paper.

Think up a story using as many flowing words as you can.

11

These words have letters which are not joined. Can you see which ones? They are marked with dots.

You have to stop and start again at the dots.

Trace over these words and practise writing them.

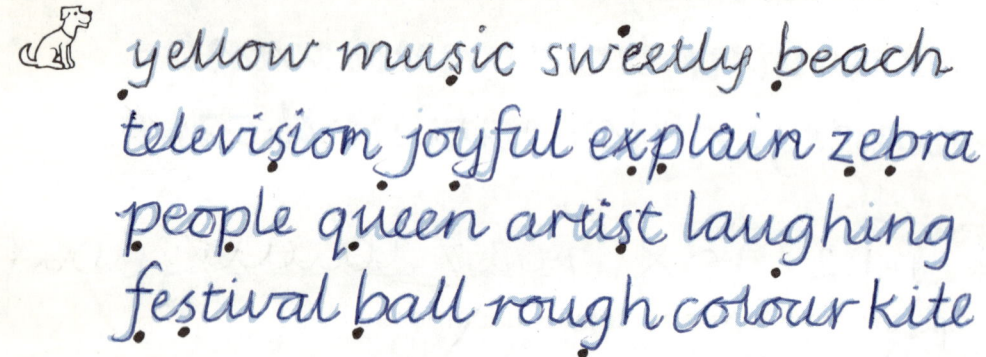

yellow music sweetly beach
television joyful explain zebra
people queen artist laughing
festival ball rough colour kite

How quickly can you write these sentences?

I heard a cuckoo calling.
Toowit too woo it went. It flew.
My cuckoo. And straight away
I knew. Brown owls don't go cuckoo.

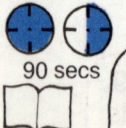

90 secs

Make up some more sentences. Use some of the words from this page, and some flowing words from pages 10 and 11.

Check your letter shapes. If they look like any of these, try them again down here.

Are all your diagonal / and down | strokes level? Are all your tall letters the same height? What about your small letters?

Here are some special cases. Trace over them.

often off

Now trace this sentence and copy it underneath.

Soft toffee is often difficult to clean off coffee cups.

ALPHABET SENTENCES

abcdefghi

lmnopqr

abc-xyz

tuvwxyz

These sentences include all the letters in the alphabet.

Copy this sentence carefully below and practise writing it quickly.

About sixty green chestnuts will make a quarter pound of very fizzy jelly.

60 secs

Here's another alphabet sentence for you to copy.

Copy this sentence below and practise writing it quickly.

The king and queen wisely decided to open the box, when out jumped a very fuzzy cat.

60 secs

It's fun making up alphabet sentences! Try to make up some of your own.

Look, Nib, this is when we go on holiday!

JULY				
Sunday	1	8	15	22	29
Monday	2	9	16	23	30
Tuesday	3	10	17	24	31
Wednesday	4	11	18	25	
Thursday	5	12	19	26	
Friday	6	13	20	27	
Saturday	7	14	21	28	

Trace over the names of the months, then copy them below.

January February March

April May June July

August September October

November December

16

> Use this page to try making your own calendar.

> Which month will you choose? Perhaps the one with your birthday?

Write the name of the month at the top. Add the names of the days down the side. Fill in the numbers.

~~January~~ August

Sunday

monday

tuesday

wednsday

thursday

friday

Saturday

Where shall we go on holiday, Nib?

Somewhere with a chip shop!

Let's make a list of what we need.

Here are Pen's holiday things. Copy and finish the list.

HOLIDAY LIST

clothes
flipflops
swimsuit
towel
t_____
s_____
c_____
b_____
b_____
s_____

18

Who shall we send postcards to? Let's make a list.

We'll need some good books to read too!

friends' names

books

Making lists is fun! Practise writing them quickly and neatly.

Here is a list of the things you could make lists of!

Your favourite popstars
Famous sportswomen and men
Countries you'd like to visit for your holiday
T.V. programmes
Cartoon characters

Follow the signs, Nib!

Did you remember your labels?

Yes, I put them on everything.

This is the label I put on my suitcase. We need to write labels like this very neatly and clearly.

Pen
Seaview Hotel
Sunnyville
Sunny Isles

Here's my label. Will you write it for me?

Now write your name and the address of a place where you would like to go on holiday.

Pen made this list of things beginning with **S**. Can you see any more? Copy and finish the list.

ROVING AIRLINES
I SPY CARD

ship
smoke

How many have you spotted, Nib?

Now make lists of the things you can see beginning with **L**, **B** and **C**.

21

"I know a poem about a walrus!"

VISIT OCEAN WORLD
LATEST ADDITION
WALTER THE WALRUS

Trace the poem, taking care with joined and unjoined letters.

The time has come the Walrus said,
To talk of many things.
Of shoes and ships and sealing wax
Of cabbages and kings,
And why the sea is boiling hot,
And whether pigs have wings.

Now copy the verse yourself.

"Now I've chosen a poem for you to look at."

Trace over the poem carefully and then copy it yourself.

*The Owl and the Pussy-cat went to sea
In a beautiful pea-green boat:
They took some honey, and plenty of money
Wrapped up in a five-pound note.*

"What do you get if you feed a lemon to a cat?"

"A sourpuss! What do cats call mice on roller skates?"

"I know! Meals on wheels!"

MON 2 JULY

Look at Pen and Nib, lazing on the beach. What do you think they are talking about? Use small, neat writing to put what they are saying in the speech bubbles.

Here are some ideas.

- Let's have a swim, Nib.
- I can only do doggy paddle.
- When is the Punch and Judy Show?
- It starts in half an hour.

Pen and Nib have gone to the fair. What are they saying? Write it in the speech bubbles.

Pen is keeping a list of how much pocket-money has been spent. Copy Pen's list and finish it yourself.

POCKET MONEY £20.00

Amusements	2.00
Ice creams/coke	1.60
Tandem hire	3.50
Disco and Show	4.00
Snacks	2.00
total	
how much left?	

Now make a list of how you think you might spend £5 in a day at the seaside.

MON 2 JULY

There are some groups of letters which often come at the beginnings of words.

Remember, some letters are not joined!

Here are some common beginnings of words. Trace over them.

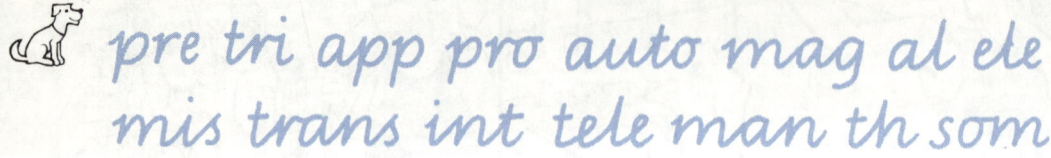

pre tri app pro auto mag al ele mis trans int tele man th som

Trace this sentence and copy it below.

Magnificent elephants appear automatically on proper television programmes.

Try making up your own sentences with words which begin with these groups of letters. Here's mine! You can copy it if you want to!

I always prefer eating triple helpings of trifle.

26

There are lots of common endings for words, too.

Trace over these common word endings.

ing ough ght ion less ible ade
lly ism able age ence ness ain
ter ent ful ler sion ory val tle

Trace this sentence and copy the sentence below.

We went on an incredible roller coaster and a weird ghost train.

Make up your own sentences, using as many of these word endings as you can. Here's my first one!

I usually enjoy Saturday mornings chasing postmen through impossible puddles.

27

> I smell fish and chips!

> Nib! Nib! Where are you?

> I've lost Nib.

> I hope this notice will bring him back.

Pen has lost Nib and is going to put a notice in the shop window. Write Pen's notice here.

Nib has been found by Pip. What do you think they are saying?
Fill in the speech bubbles neatly.

Pen is very pleased to see Nib again and has written to thank Pip for bringing Nib home.

"I used my very best handwriting, left spaces all around the letter and wrote in neat lines."

"And left spaces between words."

Seaview Hotel
Esplanade
Sunnyville
Sunny Isles

Dear Pip,

Thank you for finding Nib for me. It's good to have him back. Will you meet us for lunch tomorrow? See you in the Cockerel Café at one o'clock.

With best wishes,

Pen

Imagine that someone has helped you, like Pip helped Pen and Nib. Write a letter, thanking them.

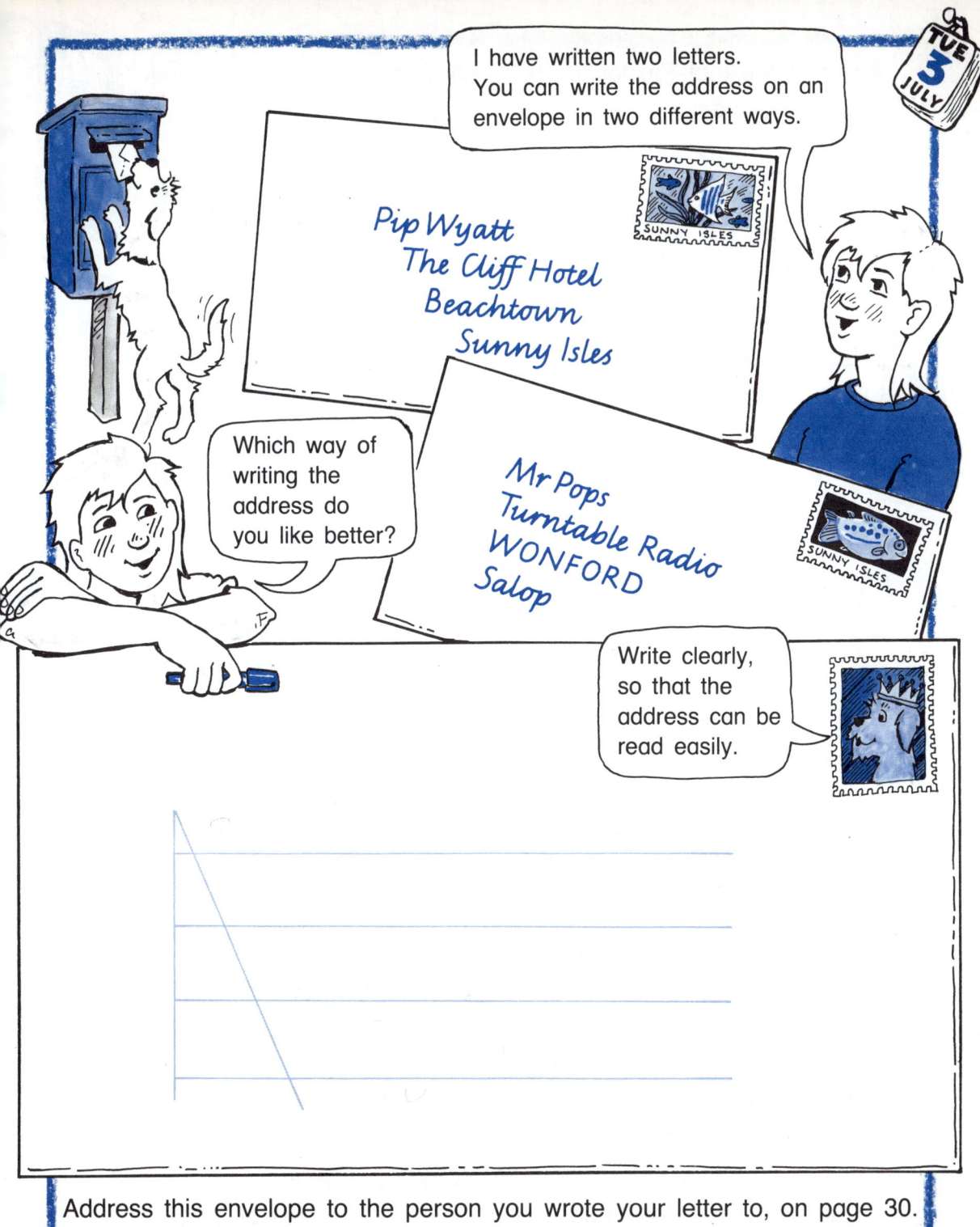

I have written two letters. You can write the address on an envelope in two different ways.

Pip Wyatt
The Cliff Hotel
Beachtown
Sunny Isles

Mr Pops
Turntable Radio
WONFORD
Salop

Which way of writing the address do you like better?

Write clearly, so that the address can be read easily.

Address this envelope to the person you wrote your letter to, on page 30.

31

WED 4 JULY

Pen and Nib met Pip for lunch at the Cockerel Café. Here is the menu.

COCKEREL CAFE

SEAWEED SOUP
FRUIT JUICE
SAUSAGES AND CHIPS
EGG AND CHIPS
FISH AND CHIPS
HAM SALAD
CHEESE SALAD
SAND BURGERS
APPLE PIE
ICE CREAM
ROCK CAKES
TEA/COFFEE
COLA

What do you think they ordered?
Write a list for each of them, as if you were the waiter taking their orders.
Now try making up a menu for a special meal, or party.
You could decorate your menu, using some of the ideas on page 41.

After lunch, Pen, Nib and Pip went for a walk on the pier. They had their fortunes told. Here are two fortune cards. Can you tell whose they are?

> You are a kind and thoughtful person, always ready to help.

> You follow your nose and make friends easily.

Here are some more fortune cards. Make up a fortune for Pen, and one for yourself.

33

SAND PICTURE COMPETITION

GET YOUR BADGE TO ENTER

Nib, everyone who goes in for the competition gets a badge.

Sunny Isles Sand Competition
PEN ENTERED

You can make badges for all sorts of things. They can be any size, or shape. Here are some ideas. You could trace them off these pages and finish them.

My favourite JOKE
Lift flap to find answer

Support the BLUES

The Punch CLUB and Judy

34

Here are some more ideas for badges. Trace them off the page and make up your own badges.

I have been a visitor to ISLAND ZOO

Here is a list of the things you could invent badges for.

your school swimming team
a summer fete
your club
a sponsored walk
your favourite charity

35

THUR 5 JULY

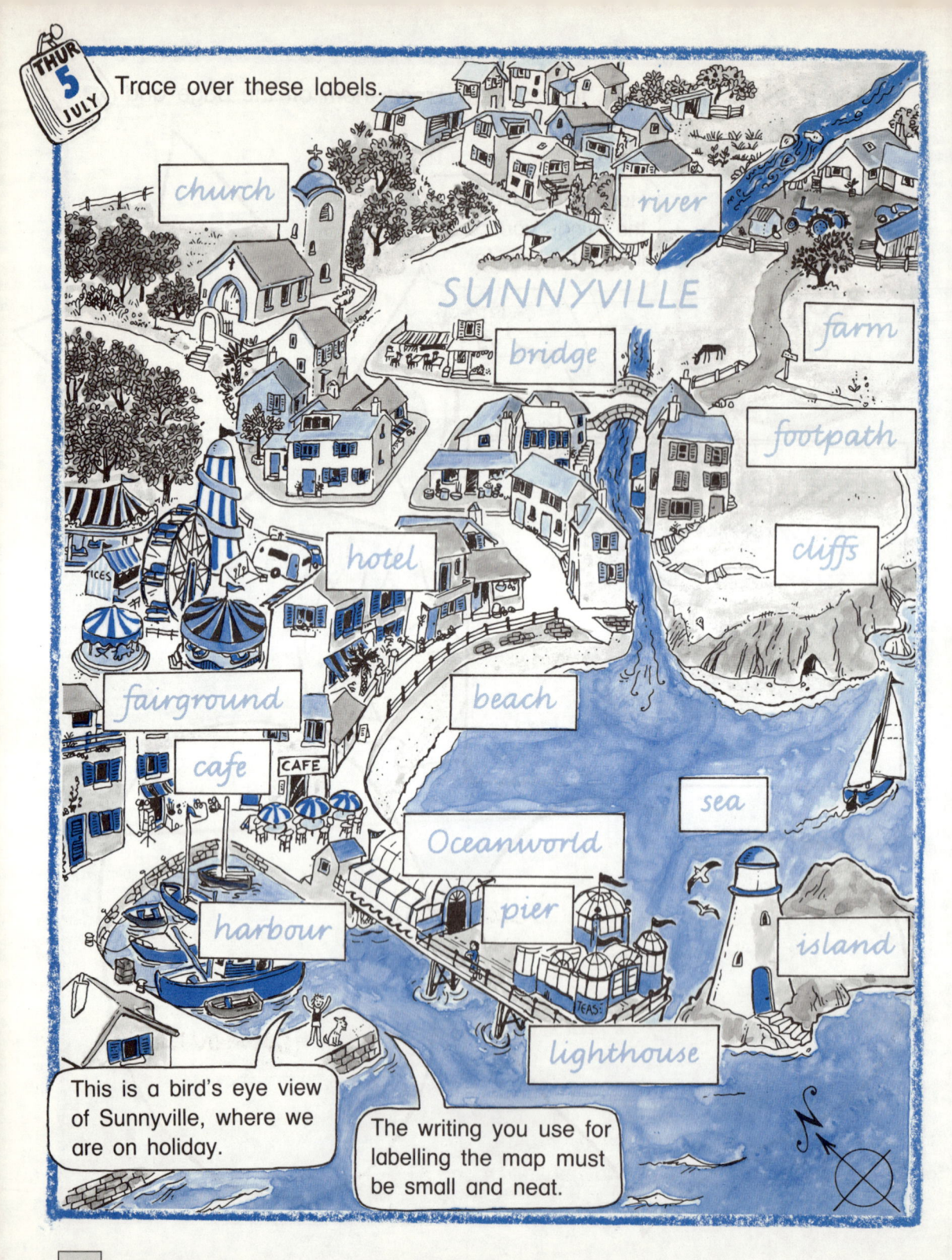

Trace over these labels.

SUNNYVILLE

- church
- river
- farm
- bridge
- footpath
- cliffs
- hotel
- fairground
- beach
- cafe
- sea
- Oceanworld
- harbour
- pier
- island
- lighthouse

This is a bird's eye view of Sunnyville, where we are on holiday.

The writing you use for labelling the map must be small and neat.

36

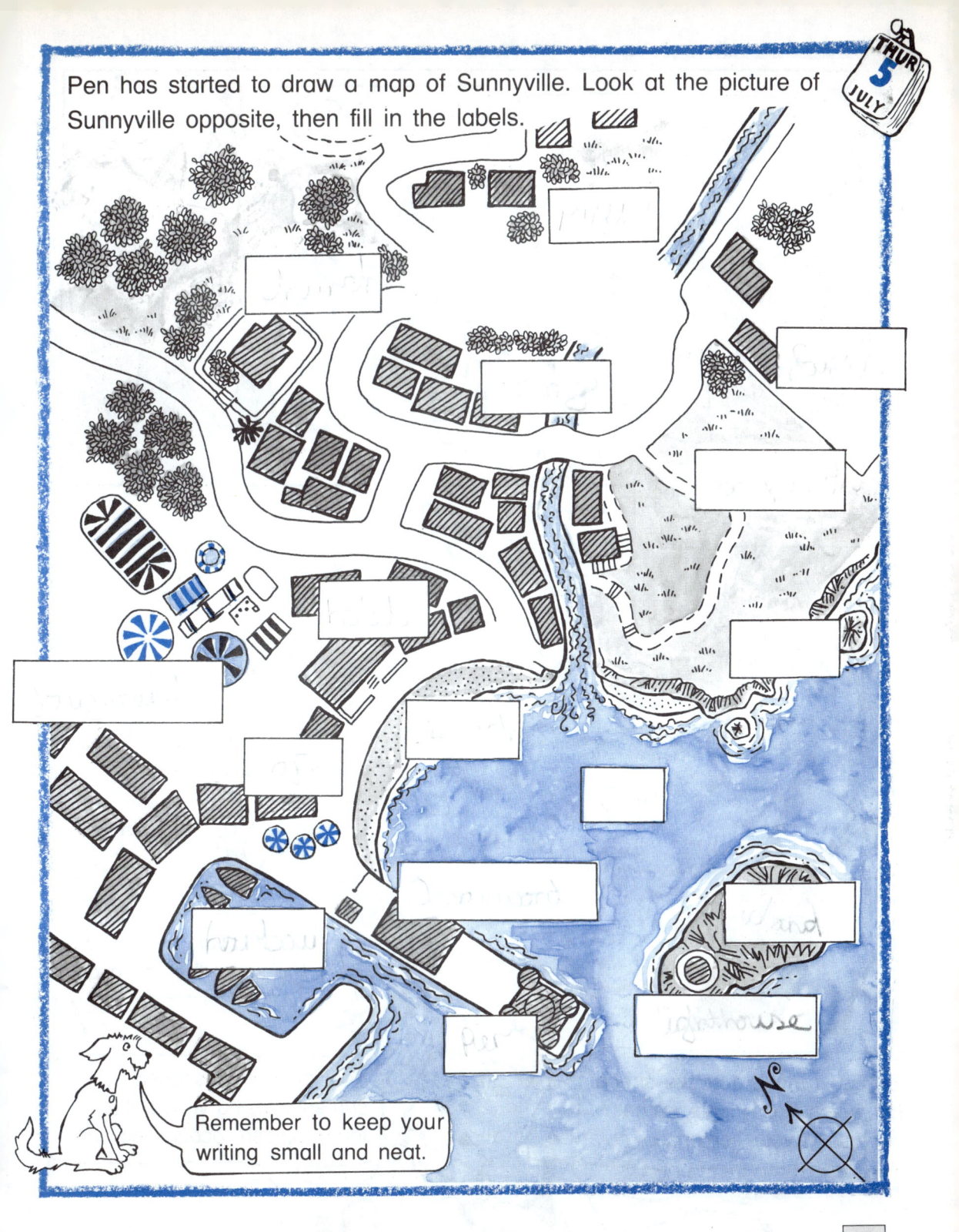

Pen has started to draw a map of Sunnyville. Look at the picture of Sunnyville opposite, then fill in the labels.

Remember to keep your writing small and neat.

37

Look, Pen, there's going to be a fireworks display tonight!

TONIGHT! GRAND FIREWORK DISPLAY HERE 5 JULY

Here's a catherine wheel made from a sentence.

The catherine wheel goes round and round showering sparks and flashes of light, red and green and glowing brightly and spreading out and yellow and blue and green.

You could copy it, drawing a spiral first, as a guide.

You could make a snake shape. Use words like wriggle, slither and hiss in your sentence.

Yes, or a wave-shaped sentence using words like foam, splash, ocean and crest.

38

THUR
5
JULY
HAPPY Holiday TO YOU
Look Nib, it's brilliant!
I know! Let's make some more pictures using words.
That's called a calligram. Here's another one.
Try making up your own calligrams. Use a pencil outline to guide you.

FRI 6 JULY

"When we get home, I'm going to have a party."

"Let's make the invitations now!"

Copy Pen's invitation card and put your name in the space.

Pen and Nib invite

_____

to a homecoming PARTY

on _____

Bring your favourite record!

"Design an invitation for a party you would like to have. You could use a different shape, if you like."

You are invited to PIP'S BIRTHDAY PARTY 3rd Aug 4-6pm

Sarah Please come to Rana's fancy dress PARTY Saturday 28th July 3-7pm

40

FRI
6
JULY
You could make your invitation look really special by using some of these patterns.
Or you could try some of these pictures.
You can unpack, Pen. I'll deliver these invitations.

Can you see the labels Pen has put on the party food?
Make up labels for your favourite party food.

You could make some place labels, to show everyone where to sit at the table, like we did.

Can you remember what Pen and Nib did on their holiday? Look back and see, then fill in Pen's diary. You could try keeping a diary of your own. Copy the diary page onto a separate piece of paper, then write down what you do every day.

JULY

SUN 1	Flew to Sunny Isles. Hired a tandem. Went for a picnic.
MON 2	
TUES 3	
WED 4	
THU 5	
FRI 6	Flew home. Made party invitations on the plane.
SAT 7	

Keeping a diary is like writing a letter to yourself. Remember the tips on page 30.

Trace over this sentence and write it below.

Nib's first swim in the sea at Sunnyville.

Now test your speed.

Write this sentence in 20 seconds.

20 secs

Looking at holiday photos is fun.

Now try it in 15 seconds.

15 secs

44

Write the labels for these photos from Pen's album by copying the words below them.

Pen and Nib fun photo

Arriving at the airport

Pen having a nap

Sand picture competition

Watching fireworks

Playing ball with friends

45

"You could try using an italic nib."

"Italic nibs have square ends, like this."

Copy the joined up alphabet below.

abcdefghijklmnopqrstuvwxyz

Now the capital letters, numbers and useful symbols.

ABCDEFGHIJKLMNOPQRST

UVWXYZ 1234567890 ';'£?!

25 secs — On a separate piece of paper, try writing the joined up alphabet in 25 seconds.

"Use your italic nib to try some flourishes, like these."

My holiday in SUNNYVILLE Sunny Isles

"I've made a scrapbook all about our holiday and I've decorated the cover like this."

"How about making a calligraphy scrapbook, where you could keep samples of all the different styles of writing you have learnt?"

My visit to LONDON

Written and compiled by Julius Caesar

The TREES in my TOWN
A. Forester

An introduction to the OWLS OF BRITAIN
Andy Fowler

"You could use some of these ideas to decorate books of your own."

"You could even make your own booklet by sewing or stapling sheets of paper together."

Make three holes.

Stitch the sheets together like this.

Tie a good knot and snip the ends.

47

Look at my long list! I have mixed up all sorts of animals, with different sorts of dog.

Can you make two separate lists, one of all the sorts of dogs in my list and one of all the other animals?

giraffe	scottie	lion	setter
collie	weasel	alsatian	tadpole
poodle	bullfrog	tiger	corgi
spaniel	terrier	gorilla	retriever
terrapin	bushbaby	panther	possum
lizard	airedale	greyhound	chow
bear	cat	bulldog	kangaroo
monkey	badger	dalmatian	

Then you can write down what sort of dog you think I am.

I hope you've enjoyed learning about writing with Nib and me.

Don't forget to keep practising!

48